WORSHIP LEADER HANDBOOK

For worship pastors, leaders, music directors, or whatever your email signature may say.

I've known Nathan for quite a few years now, and through them all he has played many roles in my life. He's been a friend, mentor, leader, and a pastor to me and I couldn't be more excited about him finally releasing a composition of the way he so passionately leads. Worship Leader Handbook is an incredible set of tools that I believe any leader within worship can grow with and obtain the ability to lead others to grow far beyond just the weekend platform.

-Chris Patterson, Worship Pastor, Mission Community Church, Arizona

Nathan is one of my favorite people on the planet… and I've met quite a few in all walks of life. What I love most about Nathan is, well, Nathan…and God-in-Nathan, streaming love, encouragement, insight, grace, and open invitation into the world. Nathan is authentic. Nathan is talented. Nathan is inspiring. And Nathan loves people. That's why he does what he does, and that's why he's written this book. So, step into the pages and let God begin to grow your heart and your vision.

- Shelley Drake, Pastor, Writer, Song Writer, Counselor, and Lover of Jesus and People.

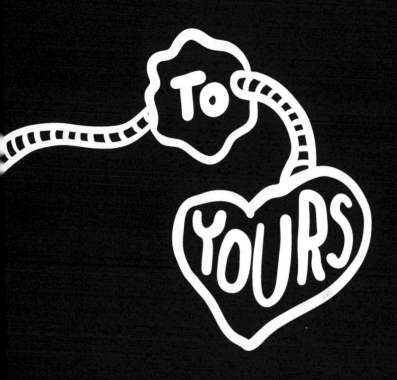

I may not know you personally, but I believe in you.
And I believe that God is not done with you. What
you're doing matters. The late-night conversations with
team members, the last-minute lyric or sermon notes
edited at the 11th hour, the pastoral conversations
with that volunteer whom you're calling up into
greatness, and the weight on your shoulders to create an
environment where the hope of Jesus is the focus.

Just remember: It all matters, and it's worth it. You're
worth it. We are all worth every moment of growth and
love and struggle and challenge.

-NDT

Contents

I wrote this book as a collection, not as a chronological study—meaning that you can read it straight through or you can jump around. I've done my best, with a little help from my friends, to put this into a format that makes the most sense—five chapters, based on some of the most commonly asked questions I get when meeting with worship leaders and pastors.

FORE

WORD

Hey Nathan!
I know this is totally random. But, I'm a worship leader in town and I wanted to see if you'd want to connect at all. Coffee? My treat? -Chris

That was an email I sent years and years ago to someone whom I stalked online after finding his photo on a church website. He had a ton of tattoos and led worship at a conservative church. My brain couldn't put those two ideas together without making my eyes cross. So, I had to meet this guy.

To be honest, I've sent a bunch of these kinds of emails out. Most of the time, I never get a response and I'm left wondering if the person on the receiving end thinks I'm a huge dork and is in their office moments later with the rest of their church staff huddled around my printed out email laughing at me … am I the only one who thinks like that? Don't answer that question.

But, unlike most emails of this kind that I've typed and sent flying out into the ether of online communication, this one got a response:

Hey Man! I'd love to! -Nathan

Thus began a relationship with someone who has walked with me through incredibly hard seasons. Someone who has challenged me to grow and encouraged me in my low seasons. Someone who has become a confidant, friend, and brother. In case you need a little more help on who I'm talking about, that person is Nathan Del Turco.

I've known a lot of worship leaders over the years. Many of whom never returned my emails. (I know I keep bringing this up but, trust me, I'm getting counseling.). But, Nathan stands out. Nathan loves his teams in a way that's inspiring. Nathan empowers people in a way that makes them fiercely loyal. Nathan leads in a way that everyone could learn from. In my experience, those leadership traits aren't anywhere close to being a given, but they're clearly evident in Nathan. This book is more than good ideas put to printing press. I've had the privilege and honor of watching Nathan personally work out the very things he's offering to you in the Worship Leader Handbook.

I've been on the other side of the tough conversations he's had to have with people on his teams. I've walked with him during seasons of him receiving unjust criticism, and then watched as he offered those same people love and forgiveness, despite being deeply hurt. I can attest that everything he has to say is more than just head knowledge, but a deep-rooted understanding that can only come from the trial, error, and victory of a time-tested worshiper … notice, I didn't say worship leader?

I encourage you to take what's written here, pray over it, process it with other people, and then circle back and do it again. You have so much to gain from the wisdom in these pages.

And after you've done all that and you find yourself empowered to be a better leader than you ever thought possible, pause for a second, and then go send Nathan lots of money. Or, at least have him guest speak at your church with an honorarium. I'm just kidding! (But, if you'd like to do that, please email booking@nathandelturco.com)

In all seriousness, though, after you've read this book, go and lead your teams well. Go and represent Jesus to a world that desperately needs Him. In the words of NDT "Own your lane and occupy it well." That's why Nathan wrote this book—so that you could be the leader you want to be and the leader your teams, church, and community need you to be. Every day, people are desperately searching for what we so freely have in Christ and we owe it to the world to be the best we can be. We owe it to the world to be who God says we are as pastors, leaders, music directors, or whatever it is you do. And this book will help you get there.

Chris Misterek
Hillsong Worship Pastor
Huge Nathan Del Turco Fan

INTRODUCTION

a little about me + why I wrote this book

INTRODUCTION

When you're talking leadership, everything starts with the leader. As John Maxwell says, "Everything rises and falls on leadership." That being said, it all starts with you.

In my early years as a leader, I didn't focus on growing my own leadership style or capacity as much as I should have. I focused on results through the people I was leading, and at times found myself frustrated when things didn't go as well as I had envisioned. It took years for me to realize that the key ingredient for a healthy team is a healthy leader. Much of the time I felt like a good leader; however, my inability to admit that maybe I wasn't leading well kept me from being as effective as I could have been. By not admitting my weaknesses, I was protecting my own ego, which, ultimately, kept me from growing and developing into a better leader.

I just assumed because I was eager, I was ready.

So, how do we begin?

First of all, you bought this book. Or stole it. Or someone thought you needed to read it and bought it for you. I'm good with any reason, as long as it's in your hands and you turn the pages. Reading a book on leadership is a huge step in becoming a better leader. Being willing to pause for a moment to learn something new is a great start.

In this book, I'll unpack some things I wish someone would have told me when I was getting started. It doesn't escape me that some might have offered these insights when I wasn't yet ready to listen, but it seems that most of these lessons I've learned by trial and error. My hope is that some of my mistakes can become your victories.

I believe that everyone has the potential to be a healthy leader and to lead a healthy team. This book is intentionally short, because my goal isn't to give you all the answers. I don't have all the answers, anyway. My hope is that these thoughts, lessons, and encouragements will help you start thinking about your own leadership and your leadership potential as a worship leader, worship pastor, worship coordinator, music architect, music director, or whatever your email signature says.

I'm a Worship Pastor and I've been leading worship for just over 12 years at the time of this writing. I've worked in the local church during these years, and I've had the opportunity to write music, work on albums, lead and speak at some conferences, counsel some terrific pastors and leaders, and share the platform with some of my heroes. I'm beyond blessed to get to do what I do, and in no way have I ever subscribed to the notion that I deserve this life. As my good friend, Berch, always says, "Favor ain't fair." Thank God for this! Because if favor were fair, I wouldn't have any.

I'm a father two terrific children + one more on the way, and a husband to Stacey Jean, my rock. I am still and will always be a work in progress, but I am passionate about helping other worship leaders and pastors be better at what they do. My calling, beyond a shadow of a doubt, is to champion people. This book is a culmination of thoughts and lessons that I pray will truly bless and help you on your journey to being the leader God has called you to be.

① WHERE DO I START?

(A LOOK IN THE MIRROR)

WHERE DO I START?

Before we get started, I want to make something extremely clear. You have the power to lead your team to health. The things you do and say as a leader carry more weight than you can possibly imagine. Healthy organizations, teams, and churches leave a bread-crumb trail that almost always leads back to a healthy leadership team or leader. In this chapter, we'll be tackling personal development and the importance of being the most healthy and aware leaders we can be.

The weight and power of our words

 Read James 3:5

Understanding the weight and power of our words is crucial to being a good leader. This was really brought to light for me in my time at Central Christian Church in Arizona. I was new to the team and underestimated my influence with the leaders around me. I would, in an attempt to build others up, give encouragement generously. Don't misunderstand—praise, in and of itself, is actually good! We should always be encouraging those we lead, or anyone for that matter. (We'll talk more about that in Chapter two.)

What I failed to recognize early on was that my

constant "heaping on" of encouragement was actually discrediting the sincerity of my words. And because my encouragement wasn't coupled with constructive feedback, I was also cheating people out of developmental moments that could be propelling them into higher levels of leadership.

Understanding the balance between encouragement and constructive help is a constant effort when you're a leader. What I quickly learned (and had to correct) was finding a balance of my words with my team. It's crucial that we take time to coach our teams through honest feedback. It's equally important to give them encouragement when they are heading in the right direction.

The goal is to cultivate an honest, healthy, and growing culture on your team, not just a happy one.

Have you ever had that moment when you've finished leading worship or a meeting and thought to yourself, "Wow. That was terrible," only to be stopped by a supervisor who said, "That was amazing!"? These little boosts of confidence can be great for the spirit in the moment; however, if this is the only input we get, it's not great for continued success or real growth. Remember, our words carry so much weight. When we're told over and over that we "killed it" when, in fact, we killed the environment we were supposed to be leading, the growth process is actually cheated and stunted.

Read Ephesians 4:25

This lack of balance between encouragement and critique can go the other way, as well.

If we create a hypercritical environment through our feedback, we run the risk of creating a culture of fear on our teams. If every time a team member comes off of the platform we grill them for singing flat or forgetting a lyric, we begin to create a perfection-minded and even a fear-based culture. These types of environments will always have high team member turnover, tense leaders, discouraged members, and stressed volunteers. This type of culture simply does not work.

There is a better way.

So, how do we find balance? As a leader, it's important to say what you mean and mean what you say.

What does that mean? Be someone whose words others can trust.

 Read Proverbs 11:3 + 1 John 3:18

Let me just give you a few tips:
- When you give compliments, give them because you mean them.
- When you give constructive criticisms, give them because you mean them.
- All constructive feedback should reflect a previously communicated vision/expectation. (We'll talk more

about this in Chapter three.)

- Don't give encouragement or criticism when there is a hidden agenda or when you yourself are stressed and haven't taken the time to examine why. Your stress can show in your feedback.

Being a leader whose words others can trust will, over time, create a foundation of trust. When you open your mouth to speak to your team, people will listen. Why? Because they know they're going to get truth from you, and not just smoke. This is crucial as a leader. This is the difference between having influence or not.

 Read Ephesians 4:15

Influence or No Influence

Think back to a time when a supervisor, boss, pastor, or mentor gave you personal advice. Did you heed their advice? How you answer that question communicates quite a bit about your relationship with that leader.

If you answered **"yes,"** then, most likely, the person who gave you the advice has influence in your life. And here's the thing: you gave the person that influence. In some way, that person earned credibility with you. Whether it's because you trust that person's heart for you, they have first-hand experience in what you're currently facing, you respect them, or you're simply close with that person, you have given him or her a platform of trust in your world. This person has influence.

If you answered **"no"** to the question, then, most likely, the person who gave you the advice doesn't have the relational equity to speak into your life. This person has a title to delegate tasks and work, but not a platform from which that advice can reach you. This person has authority, but no real influence.

Understanding the basics of influence, I want you to ask yourself this question:

Do I have influence with the people I lead?

I think Andy Stanley says this best: "Be a leader worth following."

Let's just be real—not everyone is a leader worth following. I've been led by some people I wouldn't ask advice from if my life depended on it. So, why is it that some people are worth following and some people aren't?

If you think about leaders you've had or currently have, what is it that moves you to look up to and listen to one and not the other? I'll list some of the common traits I've seen in leaders that hit the influence mark for me:
- Trustworthy and honest
- Consistent and clear with expectations
- Has a personal life that reflects healthy patterns
- Takes time to personally invest and speak life into me
- Values who I am over just what I can bring to the organization

Set the tone

As the leader, it's your job to set the tone. Here are a few Dos and Don'ts to set the tone, whether you find yourself in a group meeting, a one-on-one meeting, a rehearsal, or just hanging out at lunch.

Do

- Be an OWNER not a RENTER. You can't give away something that you don't own. If you're not an owner of your church's vision, and your team's vision you can't give it to anyone else.
- Be humble (and not fake humble). If you talk about yourself all of the time, you may not be as humble as you think. Practice elevating others over yourself.
- Be a good listener. Engage in the conversation.
- Be the calm on your team (this one is so crucial). People are looking to you for cues on when it's appropriate to get nervous. If rehearsal is going long due to technical difficulties, be the calm in the room. If something happens during a service, take the lead and get your team through the moment.
- When you're with team members, put your phone in your pocket or bag. Only check your phone during a conversation if you believe it to be an emergency or you're expecting a call from your spouse/family.

Don't

- Don't be late to ANYTHING. Early is on time, on time is late, late is unacceptable. (Some of you might just have to trust me on this.)
- Don't make empty promises to volunteers or staff that you oversee. Examples could be promising positions, influence, or making plans you aren't sure you can commit to.
- Don't be short or moody. It's important that our teams don't feel like we're unpredictable in our mood.
- Don't make your team feel like an inconvenience when they need something.

One last piece of advice before we wrap up this chapter—

Do everything you can to surround yourself with great leaders and friends. Doing all of this isn't any fun without people to share in the journey. If you don't know any other leaders, then take the initiative to seek some out. Buy someone coffee. Send an email to another person who does what you do or someone who does what you want to be doing. Be in pursuit of relationships that will make you better at what you do, and better at BEING you.

1. **Am I a leader whose words others can trust?**

2. **Do I have influence with the people around me? Why or why not?**

3. **How am I at setting a healthy tone on my team?**

4. **Do I invest in relationships that make me a better leader ?**

WHERE DO I START WITH TEAM BUILDING?

(TEAM CULTURE)

WHERE DO I START WITH TEAM BUILDING?

This is, by a long shot, the question I'm asked most frequently when meeting with worship leaders and pastors. No matter how many books you read or how many conferences you attend, this is the most fluid topic to tackle in being a worship leader. Why? Because the primary ingredient in team building is people.

People

People are fluid. People have lives, commitments, dreams, hardships, and other people depending on them. Some people have families, strong personalities, broken relationships—the list goes on and on.

When building a team, it's important to know that you are working with real people with real lives. You cannot build a team if you view volunteers as chess pieces. They are not there to make your dreams come true and they aren't there to help you win. As the leader, you're there to help them win.

Another foundational truth to grab hold of while getting started is that you are, in a large way, the limit to your team's success. Dang, that stings. How you lead them, encourage them, inspire them, and challenge them toward greatness means the difference between success or failure for your team.

Everyone can be a leader. The goal is to be a good one.

A healthy team starts with a healthy leader.

This is crucial! If you skipped Chapter 1, it's time to circle back!

Developing team culture

Culture is a bit of a buzzword in our "culture," and rightfully so. People join and leave jobs, teams, churches, you name it, because of culture. Culture is important. Now, for the sake of clarity, I feel it's important to point out that we aren't talking about culture in the context of people groups. We are talking about culture in relation to an environment and a collective way of doing, being, and operating as a team. This will be our filter.

In my conversations with other worship leaders and pastors, team culture is by far the main topic of our time together. In the context of worship ministry, having a healthy team culture means the difference between having a team, or, over time, losing a team.

Throughout the years I've been doing this, I've witnessed—and been a part of—healthy and unhealthy team cultures. What I've come to notice is that the teams that are the healthiest tend to have one major thing in common: community.

Team gatherings, team fun nights, team lunches, team retreats, team game nights, or simply a team meeting are all part of creating community that is lived out through coming together as a team outside of rehearsals and weekend services.

I started doing Team Nights in 2006 with one of the first teams under my care. This was during my Worship Internship in upstate New York. What I realized then, and still deem to be true today, is that community and connection are universal and timeless. People want to feel like they are connected and valued and that they are contributors to the team culture at large. I also learned that real community only comes by proximity and consistency. With all that in mind, Team Nights are one of the most important things you can do to create and maintain a healthy team culture.

 Read Hebrews 10:24-25

So, where do we start? Here are some steps to getting Team Nights up and running.

1. Schedule a gathering, and keep it simple.

This could be as simple as inviting your team to meet

you for coffee or game night at your house. The goal, in the beginning, is to build community, connection, and something to look forward to. When you're together with your team, stay present and get to know them. Pray together, worship together when you can, and eat together every chance you get. Over time, these get-togethers will bring you and your team closer. Remember, the goal is community.

Rain or Shine.

In the beginning stages of hosting Team Nights, it's crucial to stay consistent and do what you say you're going to do. That means that if you only have two people show up for the first time, make the most of it, have fun, and still do the next one! What I've found, over the years of doing this, is that certain personalities are early adapters to these types of gatherings and some are not. However, as you host these gatherings, people will begin to participate. In fact, it's important for people to see that the events are happening, even if they aren't there. Continue to encourage your team to come when they can, and to do their best to make it a priority. Over time, this will create forward momentum and a belief that team gatherings aren't something to miss!

2. Keep going and growing.

A great way to grow your team is to challenge them to invite new people who have shown interest in joining the worship team, to Team Night. This gives new people an opportunity to connect with team members outside of the weekend, as well as get a head start on building community and connections. Your team members will be your best recruiters, and this helps them share the ownership over the team.

Keep in mind that it's important for your team to know that they are valued and not just a part of your plan to grow the worship ministry. This is their ministry as much as it is yours, so you want to help them know that they play a key role in the future of this community.

When you've made it to this point in developing a healthier team culture, you'll start to see some natural leaders rising to the surface. These leaders will be the people who show up early and stay late. They are the ones who ask for more responsibility and more opportunities to be involved. Keep these people close! Which leads me to my next point ...

3. Never stop pouring into your team.

As a leader or pastor, it's crucial to pour into your team in these three ways:

Be Personal:
Know the people on your team. Know their names and the name(s) of their spouse and kids. Notice when they aren't there, and let them know you noticed.

Note: depending on the size and scope of your team/ organization, connections with every individual on your team may not be realistic. If this is the case, it's crucial that your team leaders/points of contact are owning this really well. Stay up-to-date with how the team is doing and ask for regular feedback.

Be Practical:

On your team, you likely have different types of creatives. Guitarists, keys players, bassists, drummers, designers, techs, kazoo players, or rain stick junkies. Invest in helping them grow in their craft. Here are some ideas of workshops that I've seen work. (Note: these don't have to be extravagant.)

- Keys and Pads
- Guitars
- Bass and Drums (Rhythm)
- Vocal Health
- Reading and Leading the Room (Worship Leaders)
- Music Director 101 (Talk back mic etiquette, following the Worship Leader, and Troubleshooting)
- Music Theory (Basics)
- Music Theory Master Class (Nashville Number System)

If you're feeling adventurous, you can always do some of these additional workshops for fun and to get creative minds working.

- Sketch Your Spirit Animal (Shout out to Jef Caine)
- Painting
- Graphic Design for Beginners
- Coffee 101
- The Sound in Your Closet (This works great to engage people who don't otherwise see themselves as musically inclined. The class: everyone brings SOMETHING with which he/she can use to drum or "make a joyful noise.")

Be What You Believe:

The team that prays together, stays together! Seriously! Pray with and for your team. I can't stress this enough. Your team is counting on you to set the tone. They WILL take their lead from you on this. Make sure you're stewarding this responsibility well.

4. Know where you're going, and communicate it clearly.

As you're working with your team, it's important to have something you're heading toward. No one wants to be a part of something that's heading nowhere. Here are a couple of things you can do to keep momentum moving forward:

- Own the Vision/Mission of your church and keep it present before your team.
- Cast the vision for your team and create goals to help the team move forward.
- Allow your team to create goals for the team.

- Create opportunities for people to grow and fail in a safe environment.
- Host a team retreat or go to a conference together. Spend the downtime talking and dreaming about what's ahead.
- Create original content or new arrangements with your team.

5. Let your roots go deep.

If you do these things consistently, you are on your way to building a healthy team culture. Remember: You're ALWAYS building culture. Good or Bad. If you're building an unhealthy culture, hit the pause button and change course. If you are building a healthy culture, keep at it. Stay consistent. Don't stop! Over time you'll reap the benefits of the culture you've been sowing and pouring into.

Investing in the health of your team culture will pay off for years to come. As leaders, it's important to build a healthy culture that outlives even our time on the team. If you do this, and do it well, this is where you'll find true legacy.

QUESTIONS to REFLECT ON

1. Understanding that we are always creating culture, does my team currently have a healthy one? Write out what's good, and what you see that needs to change.

2. What am I doing to help our team culture be better?

3. How can I show more value to the people on my team?

WHAT DOES "THAT CHURCH" HAVE THAT MY CHURCH DOESN'T?

Let's all just be honest for a moment. The comparison game is REAL. With videos and streaming so readily available now, you can watch the way other churches do practically everything. Especially worship/production/creative.

Let me start off this chapter by simply stating that God made you to be you. He gave you a lane to occupy. Occupy it well. When unchecked, comparison is a terrible filter to set standards or expectations for yourself and your team. It's crucial, as we build team culture, that we remember not to set unrealistic expectations for ourselves that are based on comparison. It's equally as important to not put those same expectations on our teams. They aren't another church's team, just like you aren't another church's worship leader.

The best way to get over the comparison "flu" is to start looking at what God has placed right in front of you. If your team isn't excited about what you guys are doing, you need to address one or all of these things:

Are you casting a clear vision and/or clearly communicating goals?

It's important as the leader to set the tone and direction for where you're heading. Set clear goals for what you're doing and what's ahead and stick to it! People won't stick with a leader that changes with every passing fad.

Communicate these goals to your team. Don't assume they know where the team is heading, if you haven't clearly communicated your team's vision. If you make changes without communicating vision, you will lose the trust and confidence of your team.

Are you honoring your Pastor's vision for the church?

This goes a long way. Be an owner of your church and Pastor's vision. Don't try to create something outside of where your church is heading. There's no longevity to this, and your team won't follow you in the long run if they feel like you're going rogue.

Are you trying to force your team into a style/sound/culture that simply doesn't fit them?

I see this happen all of the time. Be true to who you and your team were made to be. If you aren't Hillsong, don't try and be Hillsong. If you aren't Gateway, don't try and be Gateway. Focus on the sound of the "house" you're a part of and don't try to copy/paste another sound or culture. BE YOU.

Are you excited? People can tell if you don't love what you do.

No one wants to follow a leader who is apathetic about where they're going. If you are no longer passionate about what you're doing, you need to address that. Talk to a friend or pastor to process why you feel disconnected.

Songwriting

Another question I'm asked quite frequently is about how to write original music for church.

Like I stated in the previous section, it's important that we occupy the lane that God has called us to occupy. Not every team is made up of writers, and that's ok. However, if you do have some writers on your team, here are a few tips on how to get started.

1. Start small and stay consistent.

It's important to remember the words in Luke 16:10: "He who is faithful in a very little thing is faithful also in much." Meaning, start right where you are. When writing, two of the most important ingredients are God's Word + Real Life. Write out of where you, your team, and your church are at that moment.

2. Get feedback.

After you've successfully written what you think is a solid song, get feedback. Ask another writer or worship leader. Also, have your Pastor on board when writing songs for the church. Seek his/her input and feedback on the song and also on the theology. It's crucial that our songs communicate what we intend them to communicate.

3. Introduce them on the weekend.

Once you've written a song or two, and gotten some input and feedback/support from your Pastor, introduce it on a weekend! If it goes well, keep going! If it doesn't go well … keep going! Stay consistent and work at your craft as a team. Song writing takes time!

4. Write for your "house" first.

When developing a writing culture on your team, make sure you take care of your church first. Write songs that your congregation needs to hear. While the possibility of writing the next big worship or radio hit is tempting, remember that your first priority is ministering to your congregation. Writing songs for your congregation is powerful.

As writing picks up speed, be careful not to get locked into the comparison game of what you see on social media. Not every church HAS to release a full length original worship album to be "influential." Not every church worship album will get exposure outside of their own church. In fact, if the goal is to be influential or gain exposure, think again about who you are and who God is asking you to be. Don't forget the people you ALREADY have influence with: your church.

Be You. God made you unique. God made the individuals on your team unique. Don't get caught in the comparison game, and don't lose sight of who God created you to be.

QUESTIONS TO REFLECT ON

1. **Do I often compare myself and my team to other leaders and churches?**

2. **What are some things that I really enjoy about my team and church?**

HOW DO I LEAD THROUGH HURT or UNHEALTHY SEASONS?

HOW DO I LEAD THROUGH HURT or UNHEALTHY SEASONS?

There is a lot that can be said about this topic. The reality is that no two situations are the same, and all churches, just like all people, face different seasons in the faith journey. The factors involved vary in every situation and season. However, for the sake of being as equipped as possible, let's break this into two different scenarios. Note that I am focusing primarily on issues regarding poor leadership, civility in the workplace, and personalities.

Note: If you are currently in a season where other issues have surfaced with yourself or someone you serve alongside, I would love to help you process through this season. Please, feel free to contact me directly for consulting needs.

Scenario #1: When the unhealthy season is a result of your leadership

Start with honesty. Whether it's a lack of organization, vision, heart, or you've just been a jerk and your team has finally called you on it, it's not too late! The first step is to start with honesty. More importantly, be honest with yourself. You're not perfect, and that's ok. Here are some steps to go through in order to start the process of healing:

1. If possible, sit down, one-on-one, with the people affected by your behavior or attitude and let them share. Below are a few questions to get you started in getting to the core of the issue(s).

- "Would you be willing to help me see what I'm not seeing? I'm inviting you to share with me any concerns that you have about me or any patterns that you see in me that are disturbing, disruptive, frustrating, or discouraging to you."
- "Do you feel like what you're sharing with me seems like a pattern? If so, please help me see other situations in which I've done this/made you feel this way."
- "In what ways do you feel like I could be a better leader for you?"

When having these conversations, it's important to remember a few things. First, avoid at all costs talking about other team members in these meetings. Keep the conversation specific to the person with whom you are talking. Secondly, these questions take A LOT of humility. If you don't feel ready for the answers that these questions may reveal, don't ask yet. It will make the situation worse if you ask and then become defensive. Your goal in this step is to gather intel about YOU, not to prove yourself. Take a moment to cool down and gain perspective. When you're ready to ask, make sure you listen. Lastly, I would recommend spacing these meetings out a bit. Don't have them all back to back. Give yourself space to write down your thoughts before sitting down with another person.

2. Take some time away for a day or so and sit with the information you've received. Crosscheck it in your spirit and call one or two trusted people from outside of your direct influence. Own what your team is saying about you and your leadership and ask for additional feedback or insights. Then make three lists.

List A: Emotions or actions/reactions I heard or observed from my team

Sample Examples
- Distance
- Frustration
- Willingness to gossip
- Anger
- Hurt
- Lack of support or trust
- Apathy about the vision

List B: My own actions that have contributed to the emotions/actions of my team

Sample Examples
- Didn't communicate team changes effectively
- Constantly micromanaging
- Being secretive or triangulating (acting more like a politician than a pastor)
- Taking credit for their ideas
- Losing my temper when things don't go the way I want them to
- Holding on too tightly to a "perfection" mindset and refusing to let my team take more leadership

responsibility
- Being vindictive, cutting someone off in conversation, not listening, or pointing out someone's faults, etc.

List C: Where I think this is coming from in my own life

This could be a tough conversation with yourself, but real change only happens when we understand what's going on inside of us and then surrender our own challenges to God's love, healing, and forgiveness. It's tough to truly change something we do not admit or understand.

 Read Hebrews 12:11

3. Have a meeting with your team, all together. Bring the first two lists and talk through them. Allow your team to see that you're willing to acknowledge that you have faults and that you're owning them. If you're willing, you can even share some of the origins of your own feelings. This will help team members be more honest about themselves and their own situations.

- Ask for their forgiveness
- Communicate clear expectations
- Let them know you're committed to being a healthy and growing leader, as well as creating an environment where they can grow and be healthy.
- Ask them to extend the same grace that they would want extended to them. You're not going to

completely change overnight. You must have room to still be human and not be held hostage for past offenses.

- Give the team a way to continue to communicate with you. Invite them to let you know when you're off track or repeating the hurtful behaviors. They need to know they are speaking into your life and that you are listening. They need to know your invitation to talk was sincere. The team needs to be able to talk to the leader moving forward so that things don't "build up" again. It can be hard to be honest with the leader of a team.
- Pray for the future of the team and invite them to play a part in building the team culture.

4. Schedule regular one-on-one meetings with each person on your team to ask these three questions:
- "Is there anything I can do to lead you more effectively?"
- "Is there anything I'm not seeing that you'd like me to see?"
- "What are your goals this week and how can I help you accomplish them?"

These steps take courage! Lean in to the criticism and listen. If it's been a slow burn and you've been creating discord in your team for a long time, you should expect that there will probably be a variety of emotions surrounding the criticisms. This can, at times, make it more difficult to sift through the emotion surrounding the hurt/offense to really get to the core of the issue. What I would encourage you to do is take a deep breath

... and then open your hands out in front of you with your palms up. This is the posture of someone who is ready to listen, receive, and become a better leader!

Scenario #2: When the unhealthy season is a result of someone else's lack of leadership
(This can also apply to conflict with a peer.)

Start with honesty and "lead up." This is a difficult and sometimes extremely stressful place in which to find yourself. Maybe today you're on a team that's being led by someone who is not making good leadership decisions. One thing, right out of the gate, that I want to remind you of is to not gossip. I know it feels like the natural thing to do and I know that it makes us feel better—in the short run. However, gossip always makes things worse—worse for the situation, worse for you, and worse for the leader in question.

To start, ask yourself these questions:

Do I want to be on a healthy team?
Do I want to work on a team with people who trust one another and love working together?
Do I want to have a healthy leader?
Do I want to be trusted by my teammates and my leader?

If the answer to any of these questions is "no," then

it's time to hit pause do some self-evaluating. If you've found yourself in a spot where you no longer are working toward the good of the team, your leaders, and the church, you may need to take a step back and make sure you're where you should be.

If the answer to these questions is "yes," then you're on the right track. Now ask yourself, what am I doing to support my "yes" and what am I doing to detract from my "yes."

1. Schedule a meeting with your leader.
2. Prepare for the meeting.

Make two lists.

List A: What you have experienced and observed your leader doing that you believe is unhealthy

Sample Examples
- Didn't communicate team changes effectively
- Constantly micromanaging
- Being secretive or triangulating (acting more like a politician than a pastor)
- Taking credit for ideas that aren't his/hers
- Loss of temper when things don't go the way he/she wanted
- Holding on too tightly to a "perfection" mindset and refusing to let me and/or others take more leadership responsibilities

- Being vindictive
- Gossiping about other leaders and/or teammates

List B: How those things have impacted your morale and the morale of your team

Sample Examples

- A lack of motivation to contribute best ideas
- A loss of trust
- Discouragement
- Lack of motivation to reach our potential
- Lack of creativity
- Questioning of integrity
- Always looking for a hidden meaning or agenda when he/she is sharing new information
- High turnover
- Difficulty receiving feedback from him/her
- Feeling like any mistake will get me/others fired

3. The Meeting.

Establish at the beginning of the meeting that you would like to share a few concerns with your leader. Start your time together by praying for your leader and your team. Explain that you are doing this because you care about him or her, the team, and the future. You'll find that making an "ask" at the beginning tends to help set the tone. "May I please have your permission to share my thoughts on some things I've observed and experienced as a member of this team?"

Here are a few things to remember:

- Set the tone with your body language and voice. Stay calm.
- If he/she is an experienced leader, that person will probably already be aware that something is off. Experienced leaders can typically tell when something is not working well on their teams, even if they don't realize that they are the source of the problem.

There are two likely outcomes to the meeting:

- Outcome #1: If the leader hears what you have to say, owns it, and starts the process of healing (like we talked about in Scenario #1), then you have truly won over your brother/sister and you can start building for the future! (Matthew 18)
- Outcome #2: If your leader becomes defensive or aggressive and refuses to hear what you have to say, then the road ahead may be a bit longer.

So what do I do if Outcome #2 happens?

Let's talk it through a bit.

Like I stated in the opening of this chapter, no two situations are alike. People are complex, therefore, issues and conflict can, at times, be very complex. If you find yourself facing Outcome #2, then repeat Scenario #2, only with your leader's boss. In some organizations, depending on the model, this can feel really uneasy to do. However, the consequences of you not addressing the unhealthy behaviors your leader is exhibiting may result in things becoming much worse for you, the leader, and the team.

Take a breath. Take heart. Fight for your team to be healthy.

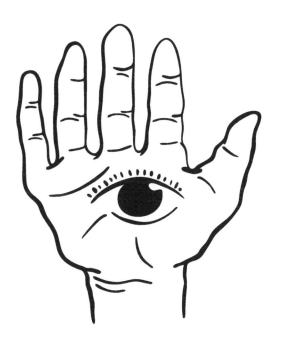

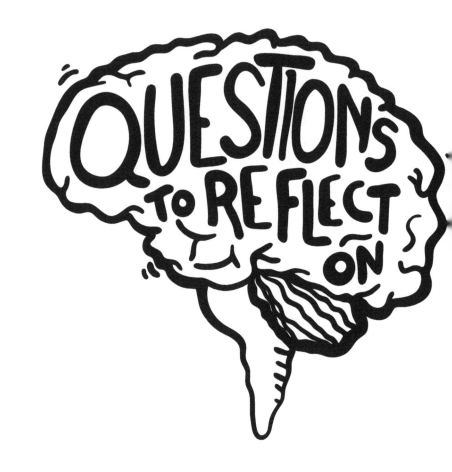

1.   **Am I currently in a healthy or unhealthy season?**

2.   **Take inventory: How am I making it better or worse?**

3.   **Do I have a friend that could benefit from this information?**

THE
BASICS

(LEADING, SETLISTS,
+WHAT to DO WHEN
the WHEELS FALL OFF)

THE BASICS

How do I lead a congregation into worship?

> _"If you can't READ the room, you can't LEAD the room."_

-Tyler Hart

Reading the room you're in is crucial to worship leading. The best worship leaders I know aren't great at what they do simply because they're dynamic singers and musicians. They're great worship leaders because the moment they step onto the platform, they instantly read the space they're in. Every space needs something a bit different. Don't mistake leading worship with simply singing songs.

Leaders, lead. Singers, sing.

So what does this look like practically? Like I've stated before, SET THE TONE. You can do this through:

1. Your body language.

As worship leaders, it's important for us to set the tone when it comes to engaging people in worship. The things we do and say on the platform give permission to the people we're leading. When we raise our hands, we're giving people permission to raise their hands. When we shout for joy, we're creating an environment that communicates "it's appropriate to shout!" So, next time you get up on stage to lead, remember—if you're happy and you know it, tell your face.

2. Inviting (Be inclusive).

"Lift your hands!" is NOT the same as "Would you lift your hands with me?" Invite people into the moment with your words. Invite them to sing with you, stand with you, rejoice with you, lift a shout of praise with you—INVITE THEM TO COME WITH YOU.

3. Reminding them why we do this.

We don't sing because God forgot who He is. We sing because He's worthy of all of our praise. We worship because there is strength found in His presence alone. We rejoice because we have reason to celebrate. We lift our hands because we understand that we need Him. Remind them!

How Do I Choose a Setlist?

There are a couple of scenarios that could be at play when choosing a setlist. Let's talk about both.

Scenario #1- Your Senior Pastor wants to give input into the weekend setlist.

First, honor your leaders. This is crucial! Remember, you have your position because your Senior Pastor allows you to have it. Make sure you give honor where honor is due.

That being said, when working with a Pastor or Teacher it's important to know that not everybody thinks the same way a worship leader might think, and that is ok! Recognizing the differences and the strengths in those differences will help you approach service planning more effectively.

Here are some tips I've learned in co-planning and communicating more effectively with my senior leaders.

1. Leave emotion at the door.

Not all Senior Leaders respond well to emotion. In my experience, bringing a well thought-out plan, accompanied by information, to the table is the most effective way to communicate weekend plans and vision to a Senior Leader.

2. Don't speak in "worship/musical" jargon.

Don't

"Hey Pastor, have you heard the new "_____" album yet? There's a song on there that's awesome! I love the way it sounds and it's got a great hook in it. We should totally do it next weekend. I think it would fit well in like a "second song" spot in the service. My friend's church did it and everyone loved it!"

Do

"Hey Pastor, I was doing some planning and I think the song "_____" would be powerful for next weekend's service. I was looking at the notes you sent out and noticed that you reference 'insert scripture' quite a lot. The song I'm talking about was taken straight from a portion of that scripture and I believe it would enhance and support the message we're trying to get across. Do you have any thoughts?"

3. Lead with "open hands."

When you bring an idea to the table, do your best not to treat it like it's your child and anyone who says anything against it might as well have called it hideous. Remember what I said about being emotional? It's a team effort to create a service. So, be a part of the team and acknowledge the fact that your idea may not always be the best one. I'll let that sink in for a moment ...

Note: If you feel like your ideas are constantly being "shot down," go back to Tip #1. Leave emotion at the door, re-evaluate the way you're approaching meetings, and try again. Many times, how you communicate the idea makes all the difference in the world whether the idea receives support.

4. Honor the call and your Pastor.

Whether your idea was the one that got picked or not, leave the room owning it like it was your own. As leaders, we bear this weight of responsibility. Don't ever, under any circumstance, bash your Senior Leader because of a service flow decision you don't agree with. Remember, you're there because he/she invited you. Be the type of leader that you want to lead.

Scenario #2- Free Reign.

There's a lot I could say on this. However, I think the main thing I want to say is to carry this weight responsibly and with honor. Acknowledge the fact that you're being trusted with close to half of the weekend's content (give or take, depending on your specific service flow). Also, remember to not be flippant with your freedom. You're designing a weekend worship experience that is speaking words of life and truth to REAL people with REAL lives. Don't choose a setlist based solely on sound. The theology we sing is of the utmost importance.

Think of it this way:

People who come into your church are proclaiming with their lips and hearts the lyrics you place before them. Make sure they are words of faith, hope, promise, and JESUS. You're creating an atmosphere in which people can borrow the faith of the lyrics they're singing.

This is your responsibility.

How do I live up to the trust I'm being given?

Be faithful and support your leaders. Make good decisions as a leader, and put your staff and the people around you before your own interests.

Don't

- Gossip about ANYONE. No one likes people who gossip ... even other gossips.
- Don't engage in office politics or triangulate for position/title. Occupy your spot and be faithful. This will allow God to elevate you when it's time for you to be elevated/promoted.
- Don't. Be. Late. (Early is on-time, On-time is late, Late is unacceptable.)
- Don't make empty promises.

Do

- Keep information confidential. Show that you can be trusted with important information.

- Send encouraging texts for no reason! Your pastors and leaders carry a lot of responsibility that you may never even know about. Encourage and elevate your pastor's spirit any chance you get. (DO NOT use this as a tool to elevate yourself.)
- Do what you say you are going to do. Be a person of your word.

What do I do if things go wrong during services?

First, take a deep breath. Second, smile. It's going to be ok! Things happen. You will survive. What I've learned in these moments (and believe me, there have been quite a few) is that honesty in MOST cases is the best policy. If tracks go out, or a mic stops working, or you drop your guitar, or a ninja runs across the stage, take a breath and do the following:

Acknowledge
If most of or the entire room noticed, say something! And keep it brief.

Re-focus
Bring the focus back to the main thing: JESUS.

Start again
Invite the congregation back into the moment.

Note: when the majority of people have not noticed something and/or there is nothing you can do to address the issue, saying something can actually be destructive to the environment. If you break a string, or your bass player runs off of the stage because he suddenly has a restroom emergency (yes, I've seen this happen), then simply stay in the moment and lead straight through it. The thing to remember is that we're always learning. Learn from any mistakes you can and do your best to prevent them from happening again.

Preventable Mistakes vs. Non-preventable Mistakes

It's important to know the difference, because it helps us learn from the situation.

Preventable Mistakes are mistakes that could have been prevented by things such as more planning, an additional quality check, some more attention to details, or preparation. Here are some examples of Preventable Mistakes:

- Tracks are in the wrong key when services start.
- Not knowing the lyrics to the song you're leading.
- A crucial piece of equipment fails for the third weekend in a row. (This one is actually an example of a non-preventable issue turning into a preventable mistake. Fix it when it breaks the first time.)

- No one is scheduled to play drums due to a scheduling mistake.
- Lyric files are full of spelling errors or the wrong arrangement is used during services.

Non-preventable Mistakes are mistakes that "just happen." You don't have control over them and they happen unexpectedly, regardless of planning or preparation.

- A person calls in sick one hour before services start.
- A crucial piece of equipment fails for the first time with no prior system issues.
- The power goes out.
- You suddenly lose your voice the night before services.
- The worship leader falls off of the stage while leading worship. #YouKnowWhoYouAre

Understanding the difference between these types of mistakes allows you to save energy and also build a healthier team dynamic. Using this as a framework/filter when evaluating services gives you a more precise way to qualify mistakes. If the service was rough due to an unpreventable mistake, there is no need for constructive criticism, only problem solving. Fix the problem and move on. If the service or event was rough due to a preventable mistake, the problem needs to be addressed, and additional conversations are most likely in order for the team member(s) involved in the service.

CLOSING REMARKS + ACKNOWLEDGMENTS

Writing this book has been a journey, to say the least. I'm grateful for the lessons I've learned along the way, and can't wait for what's ahead for me and also for you.

Like I shared in the introduction of this book, I believe that anyone can be a healthy leader and build a healthy team. It takes hard work, but it's worth it. Keep pushing to be the best leader you can be.

I owe this book, in large part to my family—who has championed me unswervingly. I also want to give a shout out to my close friends who have pushed me to put my thoughts on paper. To my Ninjas, Praise Pandas, and The Gentlemen, (you know who you are)—you make me better in everything. Thanks for never drinking my "Kool-Aid" and ensuring that I never forget who I really am— the good and the nonsense. "Stoopid" #ConnectBro

To my children Harbor Jean, Alastair Wild, and our newest addition. You are champions in every way and you have God potential for miles.
You can do anything with Jesus.
I am with you and for you. I love you.

Stacey Jean, you deserve all the things and accolades I can give you. You've been through it with me from the beginning, and I can't think of a better teammate to have in my corner. I love you.

Introduction

"Everything rises and falls on leadership." John Maxwell. The 21 Indispensable Qualities of a Leader: Becoming the Person Others Will Want to Follow. Nashville: Thomas Nelson, Inc. 2007

"Favor Ain't Fair." My friend, Berch says this often. Bishop T.D. Jakes also has a famous sermon called "Favor Ain't Fair."

Chapter 1

"Be a leader worth following." Andy Stanley. Next Generation Leader: 5 Essentials for Those Who Will Shape the Future. Colorado: Zondervan Publishing House 2003

Chapter 5

"If you can't READ the room, you can't LEAD the room." Tyler Hart, Campus Pastor at Central Christian Church, and close friend.

NOTES

Made in the USA
Las Vegas, NV
22 November 2020